I Love You to the Moon

BY MELISSA IVEY-STAEHLI • ILLUSTRATED BY RICK STEINHAUSER

Halo ●●●●
Publishing International

For more information about the author:
Please contact: Melissa Ivey Staehli
Email Author: melissa@joyfulbooks.com
P.O. Box 2552
Stow, Ohio 44224

Library of Congress Control Number: 2011915625
ISBN 978-1-935268-88-8

Halo
Publishing International
www.halopublishing.com

Printed in the United States of America

This book is dedicated to my son, Caleb, who is the greatest gift God ever gave me.

I love you

to the moon

in the sky

I love you

to the ocean

so deep

and so wide

I love you to

the rising sun

That brightens

up the day

I love you

to the forest

Where you love

to run

and play

I love you to

So very

far away

Your love is

always with me

And in my

heart you'll stay

CPSIA information can be obtained
at www.ICGtesting.com
Printed in the USA
LVIC04n0610210214
374595LV00002B/40

9 781935 268888